AF333537

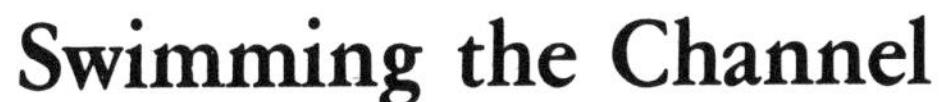

Swimming the Channel

P. O. Box 10040
Chicago, Ill. 60610

Swimming the Channel

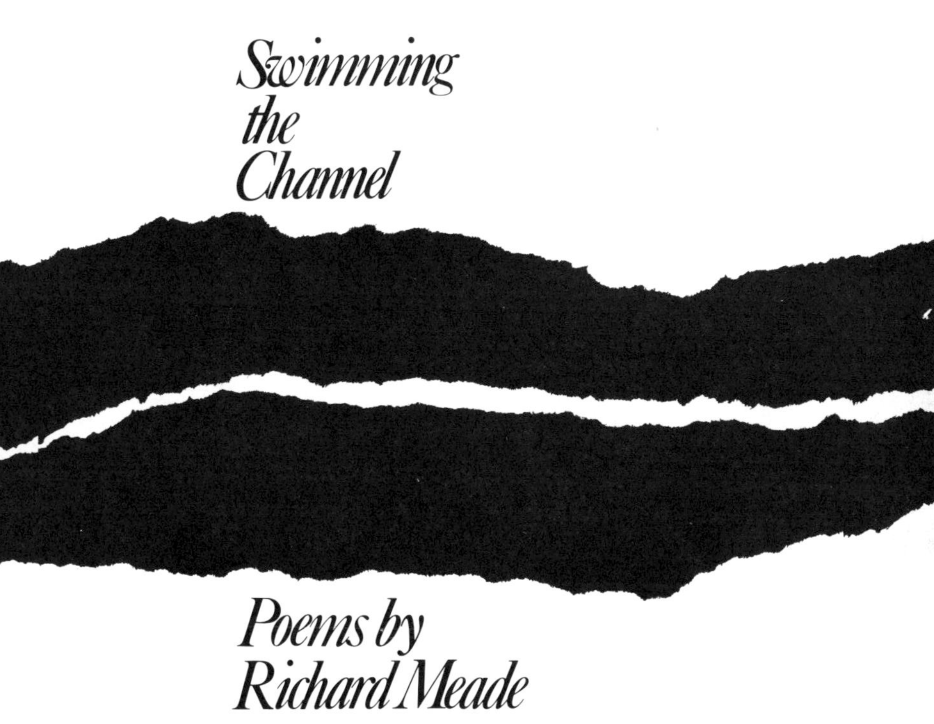

Poems by
Richard Meade

Design by Emory Mead

Acknowledgements

Grateful acknowledgement is made to the following magazines in which some of these poems first appeared: *The Worcester Review, College English, The New York Quarterly, Gob* and *The Triangle*. Several other poems were first published in a chapbook, *Portage Lake and Other Poems* (Gob Poetry Press, 1972).

Library of Congress Catalog Card Number: 80-26545

Library of Congress Cataloging in Publication Data

Meade, Richard, 1946-
  Swimming the channel.

  I. Title.
PS3563.E16856S95   811'.54   80-26545
ISBN 0-931704-07-3
ISBN 0-931704-06-5 (pbk.)

for Norbert Blei, who got me started

I sleep and my heart stays awake.

—George Seferis

Contents

Three

One

Channel Bass

I fished for years
in Michigan towns
off piers, hunched in row boats
throwing a line
from a muddy bank
to the hungry mouth of a snag.
Blue gills, perch, and rock bass,
I never caught a big fish.
Off the channel once
line dropped straight down
among rocks
I hooked a big black bass.
I hauled him up
like a boy, all muscle
and no technique.
Only the memory of anticipation
framed against those years
of unsuccess. He rose
like a dark dream
twisting to form.
I saw him beached on
the waterless edge of sleep.
My reel purred.
I thought he'd break
with a splash
but he'd had enough.
He slipped that hook
and sank like a prank
into the waters
of the lake, took up
the commerce of the deep.

I looked at my line,
the channel waves
slapped cement.
I didn't move my pole.
Instead I looked into
the green wet
where I could catch him yet
not with hook or line
or sinker
but with the extra eye
I blinked.

Prelude

On a walk
in late spring
I stop in a driveway
to look around.
A nest has fallen.
To a cat's reach
or the wind?
Death doesn't bother
with distinctions.
A shell cracked and seeping
the twisted leg
of the unborn bird
lies on the sidewalk
like a twig,
the head hidden
still sealed in that failed,
fragile armor.
The children on the block
arrive, gasping,
their eyes wide
they turn to crying.
And the shocked mothers
gather to comfort them
pulling the suburban cloak closer.
The aftermath of a minor disaster
becomes a prelude
to something greater:
the way we face the world,
struggling toward
potential flight, trying
to keep from breaking.

The Sanctuary of Aphaea

Solitary, erect as edicts,
these columns are the best
preserved in Greece.
I come here every evening
with my niece
to watch the sun sink
into their embrace
and let the girl
climb upon the ruins.
She has her Brownie
and does it for a picture.
Last night
assaulting this high hill
with folk guitars slung like
muskets on their backs,
dangling price tags
fresh from Sears, they came.
From Stanford.
Twelve countries in twice
as many days,
flying with excursion fares
in plaid Bermuda shorts
meandering like labyrinths.
They wanted hints on other
spots to stay,
complained they only had one day
and built a fire.
I watched the fire trail
swaths of smoke
across the pillars.
They offered me beer,
sang Dylan and The Stones.

For a moment
that sensual music held me
there. I pulsed with desire
for quick-limbed California
girls, thought of luring one
to bed, like Zeus,
by wile, but I left.
Now she has a picture.
The shuttlings of dusk
come soft
the sun sets and passes on.
Tomorrow I shall let the child
go alone to Aphaea
and photograph her world
as she will.

Letter from Hydra

The poets here eat nothing
but cabbage.
In fierce translation
the Germans read Kazantzakis.
For 30 dracs the school girls
will wash your socks.
The priests applaud my accent.
The Venetian cannons impose
themselves on all the tourists.
And the fishermen are photogenic
for a certain fee.

Philosophy

I knew a philosopher once.
He lived in the country.
There was a fine view of the sea
but no trees.
His shelved abstractions
kept him company.

Once day I read a letter
to his mistress
who he kept in the city.
He dealt in tautologies.
He loved the unchanging absolutes
in the same way he loved her.
And told her so.

I took a train home.
The trees repeated themselves
without getting repetitious.
My breath came and went
never the same.
I thought,
do not think of me
as a fixed and changeless entity.

On Kea

Terra cotta figurines
are gathered in crates
along this mooring

their secrets still
unwhispered to
inclement archeologists.

Out of nowhere
a sloop, smooth as ebony,
moves into harbor.

The women on it
are from Winnetka.
And since I come

from the North Shore
we compare, over ouzos,
our parkways.

Herat Summer

The season restates
its lustral virtues: the sun
splinters into shrapnel

dust sweeps up an incautious
witness, the slack tongues
of camels preclude

their savage conversation.
Only the minarets retain
their vision. They taper

toward proclamation. I close
my book and wait patiently
for some deferred conclusion.

dock

past
the raft
the moon
swims

waves
rise and
crest
slapping
the beach

cloud canvas
torn
by a moored
schooner's mast

under this
dock
the hollow
plop
of the *lake*
ticking

Valentine's Day

It is a public time
for bearing gifts
to those we love
a day to ritually admit
what we usually fear to say:
we are desperate to give
and to receive.
We wear our hearts around
like painful badges.

There is not much time
to visit your son's school
your own classes
at the university are about to begin
another philosopher will lecture
on the will.
But you come with your gift
and sit in his room
waiting for a chance
to give it to him.
His teacher turns pages
points at the map.
He is at his desk writing.

You have given him up
to his father.
The divorce has left him
needing a man more than he does you.
You can feel it in every tantrum.
At seven he wants the rough contact
the snug simplicity
of his daddy

not your burning clarity
the knowledge of what we are
and what not
you don't care what ambition dreams
but what someone will be.

You have *decided*
like the philosophers
tell us to do
but all that natural longing
protests your rational choice:
You have abandoned him
to an alien world
that knows nothing of speech.
Who will keep him from harm?
The teacher is at the blackboard
and your son looks up
embarrassed by this visit.

It is too late to wait longer.
By the time you reach the car
you are crying
starting the cold engine like
the numb heart.
Your stomach tightens.
Through the curved glass
the objective world glistens.
You push on the gas
toward a mad acceleration.
It is the end of a day
with a masculine name
meaning to be strong
and suddenly you know why
you don't care for philosophy.

Days

There are days
when you are waiting
for a train.
It is cold
and the station lobby
is locked
and the wind blows
snow across your face
that sticks in your hair.
Already the train
is ten minutes late.
You are just beginning
to reget
your habitual promptness
in the face
of a life
which is never on time
when out of nowhere
the train arrives
cuts in half the tree
opposite you
coming down like a knife
in the night.
The branches are caught
like fine lace
against a sky gray as rails.
And you have to
interrupt your misery
to observe once more
the obdurate beauty
of the world.

Holt Lake

At Holt Lake
on an island camp site
the sun going down
behind a granite treeless bluff
I walked to my canoe
and flushed a ferret
from the brush.
It moved in a slow zig-zag.
Caught in its mouth
was a long snake
writhing in the air
like some protean hieroglyph.
I stood there
paddles in one hand
and watched the ferret weave
across my path, unaware.
The wind came up
and dark waves lapped
at the edge of my pebbled inlet.
A cloud bank split
as I watched,
the ferret's low growl
just audible
in the troubled summer air.

The Way

The heart tightens
to the winter wind
the long years threaten
to collapse
sucking the body dry.
Everywhere things seem to end
where they began.
We laugh
set it all down
and turn to the land again.
But beyond the winter dark
something glows
not a light, not even reason
but walking back home
one night
it lights up the wide world.
We see again the same finish
but look at the way!
There in sudden sight
are the places we've been before
no two colors the same
blazing the journey white.

On a Ferry

I met a boatman
on a ferry.
He was what you expect
with his belly
and dirty jokes and
winks for the pretty girls.
Even a pocket flask
of — who could tell — gin?
Except for this one thing:
Next to the wheel
was a weathered copy
of Stevens,
the collected poems.
The conventions of culture
collapse around such men.
It got me thinking
about red weather.
He spoke a line
as if it was speech
for an amusement
entirely his own.
I watched the smooth water
catching the sun
in long ribbons
like polished glass
and I thought about surfaces
about the ways they reflect our faces
hiding the depth within.

Watching the Meteor Shower

At midnight
the moths rattle
against the screen door.
A light wind stirs
in the tops of pines
and remakes
the lattice of moonlight
on the ground.
Down at the beach
I am lying
in the sand
making a hollow
with my head.
It is too calm for waves.
Looking up
at the full bowl
of the August sky
I wait for it
to light up with meteors.
The papers say Perseus
will shoot them out
like Zeus in a shower of gold.

Another Night

Day shuts down
that old factory
assembling our lies.
It's done with.
The moon comes out
like a chimney fire
puffing out its red glare.
Looking for a plate of grub
soup perhaps
we find only bowls of dust.
We turn back
inside ourselves
looking for a place to sleep
but all night long
from one slab of loneliness
to another
keeping us awake
the night whistles.

The Dark Other Shore

Just at dusk
Dad would disappear
pole and pipe in hand
the canoe moving out
the tie rope sketching
a widening v.
Dinner would be done
Mother calling from camp
it was getting cold.
But before I went up
I turned to see him
small against the sky
drifting towards
the dark other shore.

Loons

On Mountain Lake
two day's paddle from Grand Marais
calm as I approach
two loons and their baby.
They skirted me to the right
went under as if to play.
The baby did not come up.
It was the fish's day.
I could see in their eyes
the blank terror
of wild things facing the unknown.
They circled in mad loops
beat the still water
with a flash of wings.
Their cry was a quivering wail.
They dove, surfaced, and dove again.
I was but a few yards away.

Moths

Beating their wings
against the mesh of screen.
Here outside the prison of the night,
the unattainable light.
And what if they should win
this dream of day
this element alien to all
they seem to be?
The steady throb of ecstasy
battering the bulb
until the broken body stills.
Like us
burning out their strength
in pushing back the dark
spinning in a bright ring
about the halo of the lamp
to shed on their dark forms
a heavenly, transforming light.

Willow

Tall and self-contained
like an aging statesman
still admired
for his remembered eloquence,
a rhetoric of hope
and growth
articulate in every ring,
a wise man full of love
gathering the yard
into a green embrace,
your crime was only weakness
yielding to age
and the weight of limbs
dropping a thick branch
in the fury of a storm
on power lines
and a man's garage.
A man's garage!
To mock and mangle
all that he's become,
to threaten
that display of wealth
which keeps him
from his neighbors:
A capital offense.
And so they come
for you
with a white machine
tall as a giraffe
not to graze silently
on fleshy leaves
but to moan with need
for your very life.

The saw cuts and snarls
the day away.
A man moves down
your trunk
taking each helpless arm
like a mad surgeon
hungry for amputations.
Gradually the sky above
opens up
and leaves a hole.
Remembering your gestures
in the wind,
your canopy of grace
this is one absence
I will not forget:
This was your place!
Looking out over
the affairs of men,
I could, like you, weep.

The Dream Path
(for Richard Jop)

Heading south
on Lake Shore Drive
the waves pounding the cement
like heavy fists of fate
sending up a thin spray
which came in
through the open window
and dampened your hair
you asked, "Feel that?"
I said I did.
And you shouted
your voice going out
to the startled joggers
and the dance of basketball
amid those netless hoops:
"Hey, everybody! We're alive!"

Now you're not.
A bad step on the canyon rim
sent you flying
500 feet or so.
No words this time,
a sorry fate for a talker.
But what about a thought
in that quick descent?
You told me once
you had no fear of flying.
It was arrogant, you knew,
but you felt invulnerable.
Perhaps it helped you then
knowing that at the end
you would land feet first
and live to tell me jokes
about this circus dive.

Luck said no.
You who knew so well
how to live
to take the measure of a day
watch the sun skid off stage
knowing this is all there is
who taught me words
the wordless Mahler had to say,
have no more.
Here on the dream path
I give you back this pledge:
Because of you
I love this life,
because of you
I won't forget to be afraid.

Swimming the Channel

For a small boy
swimming was a shore line thing.
Sand bottom under foot
the easy reach of raft or ladder.
Close to the pier
sun filtered through
turning the small shells green.
Sticks and stones
were the bottom things
you dove for.
You stood as much as you swam.

The channel the forbidden thing
your mother kept you from.
Ferries steamed through
to dock at the old hotel.
Sailboats sought it out
wanting the wider wind of the big lake:
It was deeper than any dive.
Waves tore the surface
and made it churn.
Ladders eased you down the cement side.

You climbed into the black
like a boy going into a cave.
There was no shore line here
beneath your feet
only the startled fishes.
Swimming was what you had to do.
You pushed out
face down, gathering breath,
water clouding your eyes
no light
seeking the other side
like an island after shipwreck.
Knowing as you did
catching a glimpse of sky
that this could make small boys big
though you couldn't say really why.

Two

Boca Grande

The beach
in this moonlight
finds the eye
straining against itself
to see.
It's a battle
against clouds and shadows
the sand and water
mottled this time
in patches of bone white.
But there is light enough
to see the fishing fleet
the single lamps
forming sea-bound constellations
and the hum of engines
is just enough
to make you fear invasion
and lean on me
your mind darkened by
palms and banyans
and make of our life
a science fiction movie
waiting
hands clasped
for another alien landing.

The Capture of Passion

It is a story told to me
more than once.
Several adventurers enter
a dark thicket.
There is no sun there
only this heat, this trouble,
this closed circle of surround.

They bring nets.
The mesh is opened
hung in trees like a canopy
of sleep.
A bow hums, an arrow flies,
the net drops.

Back home
passion is displayed
in the public square.
There is a motto etched
in the base of the wooden cage:
Pity us this.

Passion stalks through the long night.
Her roar is heard in distant villages
that have no moon.
Toward morning there is sudden panic:
Her cage is on fire.

Winnifred's Discovery

Where were you
when that shy discovery
crept through the quiet path
in your night?
Were you baking
with mounds of dough
like a fortress in a steamy kitchen?
Or standing at a crosswalk
the yellow caution light
dimmed by the flare
that marked your find?
Or only somewhere reading
suddenly aware of the calm
fragility of ice?
I know you are afraid.
In the world you have entered
nothing is easy.
Wait for things to be said.
When they are spoken
they will show you
where to go.

In Back Bazaars

In back bazaars
in Delhi
we bickered
like bluejays
turning the dark eyes
of laborers
cycling to prayers
and a gourd
of boiled rice.
Finally we settled
on a price
and bought that sari.

Now, three years later,
driving in rain
in Ann Arbor,
past freshmen
rife with beads,
in a boutique
sheik with the fashions
of the East,
I see your sari.

I think of it
now locked
in that mute New England
trunk, falling
like green waves
in an attic
and my face constricts.
This woman steering me
back to her warm duplex
asks if I'm sick
and I say:
just a little
in the halting traffic.

The Persian Earrings

It took me
two hours
coughing in dusty shops
sipping tea
and sharing secrets
before Hakim
slow with surrender
gave up those earrings
for a price
I could pay.

Sharyn, her eyes bright
with craving,
says there's not
another pair.
She moves in my mind
like a wrestler
battering poor jewelers
and rattling their
eyeballs.
Did you see her freeze
when you walked
into the embassy
and dangled diplomats
from those golden threads?

When I dream of you,
it is with
the earrings.
You are floating
down stairwells,
the magic of Persia
at your earlobes.
Hypnotic like opium
you cast your spells
on strangers
and in your haste
they love you.

Virginia Days

The flesh awakens,
shocks us out of sleep
bones pressing bones
breath like the last summer wind
going to fall
the body's edges
weathered by the night epoch.

There are reasons for such wakings
the gray ridges shading to blue
leaves falling down valleys for miles
turning once.
Now it is noon.
Beneath us stone pillows your head
the sun on my back our blanket.

The rocks pool us in basins
and turn our story
into green lichen
capable of getting by
without much water.
Years later
revisionist geologists uncover
our imprint
construct a theory
reflecting our buried kind of truth:
a dynasty of days.

Surface

You drift through the surface of a life.
It is windless outside.
In the thin things exposed to air
not much movement.
You take a vacation to Florida.
Your husband wants you to tour the coast
in a glass bottom boat.
That way you can see coral, sand crabs,
the flashy colors of darting
but directed fish.
When you look down, there are no fish.
Only me
drifting beneath you
reaching up to touch,
leaving a dark handprint
everywhere you look.

Orator

You orator of second chances
spinning out these fantasies
of the future
across the breakfast table.
How do you manage
to avoid seeking out
what you will be
in the dead ends of the past
steering a sure course
toward tomorrow
without ever looking back?
You told me once
when I mentioned a truth
that you needed
the illusion of hope
and pushed back my words
like the dark of a forest,
giving wider space
and clear directions for
one departure to another.
When the tears came
I knew that you were right.
I knew my truth
was your catastrophe
and I stepped up
on your soapbox
adding my clamor
to your argument of hope.

Memory and Music

Memory, that knife,
needs only music
the lute of de Narvez
on an album you gave me
to pierce the flesh
and cut the heart.
Out of the notes
those strange lost images
of the past
float by carrying
their jumbled emotions.
Here on a steamy summer day
I try to imagine love without pain.
I think of the birthday
greeting you sent me,
"All my love forever."
as if it were some
historical truth
I could trust
written on the distant continent
of our shared life
now drifting like fog
across the bog my life has become
since you have been gone.

Far and Forever

We are in bed
in the dark and
you say you love me
and because it's dark
you don't see
the tears or know
that when you say that
I have to cry.

It's not normal
you would tell me
but I can't help it
when you go away
to work to ski to shop
I am afraid
imagining the silence
of the world without you
wondering if.

I try to write
but I can't
surely there is something
the matter
only my thought is
protecting you
I try to keep you safe
but by yourself
you are out there
alone
with the hazards of the day.

They wait for me
to let down my guard
to take you
far and forever from me.

Naked

You come to me naked
shimmering
like the trees in rain,
your arms folding and unfolding
their secrets
your hair shining
with the half light
of an alien moon,
your lips in the feathery flight
of quick small birds.
Beneath your bare feet
the leaves crackle
and begin to burn.

Your heart unfurls
like the leaves
and the wind sends
those sharp reminders
through the skin
into the heart
which is naked now
for the first time
waiting like a promise
to be kept.

I pull you close.
There are storm clouds
gathering inside me
and in a while
the wind and rain come
and pierce the skin
with the jagged blades of desire.
I move out over the new terrain
of your body
hearing only the long low moan
in your throat.

Pocket Chekhov

When things go wrong
I can't seem to hold together
the bits and pieces
I pick up the book
you gave me
the pocket Chekhov
thumb through the waiting pages
looking for whatever I lost
in the gully of a bad week.

You tell me
that when it happens to you
you can't read a love story,
you don't read at all
pushing the dead heart deeper.

But these stories
are not about love,
but about the spaces in between.
Pulling ourselves up
the ladder of the heart
we try to deny our separation,
but there is no escape
from the shores of the given
on this imperfect globe.

Texas

Once, in El Paso, under the bridge
I watched small children huddle in sleep
on the cement floor of a washroom.
I was teaching English to their parents.
In the night, they took over my dreams.
More about Texas I do not know.
Dust, cowboys, oil rigs
pounding the ground?
Is the range open or closed?
It takes an awkward form now.
No longer large, I take it in my hand.
It has the shape and weight of longing.
There is this reason:
it is where you are.

The Painting of the Week

is abstract
and I am like the lecturer
talking too much
betraying your silences
with words
this appetite for explanations.

I must try to learn
your empty places
like those in paintings
watching the fingers of a hand
in a careful tracing.

I have misunderstood
the sentences you begin:
they aren't meant to be finished
but to trail off
in wordless conclusions.

This Time

I love you so, she says
and clings to me as if
I were a twisted pine on a mountain ledge.
Here shoulders quiver
she is either cold or scared
and her arm
stretches across my chest like a fallen branch.
Her hand is on my neck.
I can feel your pulse in two places, she says,
counting your heart as one.
In the still air of the room
my pipe smoke still lingers
though the pipe has been out now
for a long time. On the ceiling
I watch the light change.
It is six o'clock
and ever so little dusk climbs the wall
coming in through the band of window
between the improperly drawn curtains
which are green.
Just this time is enough, she says,
I can feel it passing. And there's
no reason to get up.
My hand moves down her back
each vertebra is a sleeping stone
on a mountain path.
And still she clings
as if below were the ravine
of her other life
and to let me go would be
to tumble down and fall
for a long time
before the brambles cushioned the thud.

Cynthia Leaving

Mountains map
the most uncertain
of separations.

You acclaim the sunlight
and solitude now,
beyond the wrinkles
of Colorado.

The storm clouds I gather
here are heady fortresses
that never shower forth
their arrows.

They say Denver is too high
for rain.

You go
not like a doe
whose tense vibrations

record precisely who is there
and who is not

but like a lynx
whose weaving run
measures nothing but retreat.

I think of your flight:
it stretches the silence
between us.

The Dawning

It slips under sills
fingers our thighs
hesitates on wrists
like suicides.
Saber rays strike
the bureau: dust fidgets.
It's always the same
with you, Susan.
Outside you hear
the squirrels chatting
their gossip,
the wind cry of miracles
waiting to be born.
The perfect word forms
in your mind,
begins some reckless poem.
Once more I'll put
your rhymes away,
pull dark shades
against the morning,
kindle brief fires
out of pencils.
I'll take the new poem away
and begin to touch you,
our dark day dawning.

Toward Morning

Toward morning
the sea severed
that bloated moon
we prayed to.

On the hill
a greedy goat
munched the boundaries
of our heaven.

We were lying
in a dump. The limp stones
that scattered sleep
were tin cans.

The flies sucked
at our empty wine bottle.
When we fled
they knew why.

Covert

Concealed, disguised
in *hunting,* a hiding place
for game
but here in
the hollow thicket of desire
is no shelter
we are on an open plain
watching dusk
settle on the day
like an owl
waiting for dark to strike.
Our bodies remain
tiny points of light.
The evidence is all about
on our hands and lips
you say you can gather it
leaving nothing
the arched room swinging free
no traces.
But now that you are gone
the room is giving me back your pieces:
a glasses case, a belt from your dress.
Nothing here will hide you.

Alone

Mourning the loss of night
you fight back the day
with tears salvaged from dreams
and a wall of sheets.
This is the way you want to be alone
with birds like alarm clocks
ringing outside your bedroom window.
It is your bed, not mine,
you remind me
and you can cry there when you want.
But you're like a map
folded the wrong way.
The road you began on leads you astray.

The vehicle of day lumbers on.
It is still raining
and pulling back your sheets
I find you drawn up like a child
seeking familiar spaces
your hands clutching kleenex
like small tools.
You try in a near sleep
to turn on the pocket flash
but your thumb never finds the switch:
not here, not now, not this way.

The Brady Farm

When the knot of fear
tightens on our country pleasure
and your eyes are glazed

with claims that kindle
in the embers of our touching
I have to blur your face

rise on ripples of myth and
memory to some distant place
of certitude. I see

you a chimera then.
Nothing of the look of
liege and lies invades your

features when that beast breathes
its hot assertion:
love will never catch us

as we are,
couriers detained, heavy with
history for someone else's ears.

Like carolers at midnight
we herald no one
but ourselves.

What You Fear

It is the self at rest
peering in
through the window
of the body
the dark pool
all stillness within.
Shadowy figures like fish
gliding beneath
watching the unbroken surface.
It is the lack of effort
the way we move
shedding the dead weight
of the mind
like stone
turning the puzzle pieces
into solid form.
It is the moment.
It could be repeated
even expected
and certain vestiges
words, for example, or logic
might be abandoned
at the edge
all the known methods
of movement
slipping away from you.

Young

We were young then
spilling out
of the dream of childhood
sifting the days
through our hands
like fine sand.
We didn't fear
the dare of the future
breaking at our knees
on the wind-driven shore.
Through the slow unfolding days
we marked our growth
on tall straight pines
with a notch to show
the triumph
of our increasing height.
But we reached a time
when we were no taller.
It was a shock.
We were to be
no more than we were.
We had to take
the measure of a life
in unseen ways.
The stars were thrown out
against the sky
like scattered tacks
and after a moment
poised like sculptors
above a marble slab
we gathered them up
and stuck them
in the map of destiny.

Three

Games

You are composing and recomposing
a letter to your dissertation adviser
striving for just the right touch
of humility.
In the book I'm reading
the heroine tells of her time
in graduate school
cultivating the proper deference
that would win her fellowships.
Even the student
behind the towel booth in the gym
is well practiced.
He has mistaken me for a professor
and apologizes for calling me
by my first name.
Everywhere the same dull game
of sycophancy.

Walking back to my car
I pass the art museum.
It is cold and gray in March
but on the lawn
two girls unfurl a blanket.
They pour lemonade from a thermos.
I am amazed.
Their winter picnic is about to be
a success.
It's my move and I can hardly remember
the rules
for this afternoon game
of wonder.

Event

Someone to talk to, she said
amid the journalists,
wry objective men
given to observation
of the things that pass
easily between hands.
Strange that in that hour
geared for laughs
and regional truths,
they touched that other one
somewhere between glance and gesture.
Later he held her.
Now the moon has rounded the globe
more times than he can remember,
a circle of tribute to choice
and chance, to the two of them
lost in what they have found.
He watches in Illinois.
She listens in Texas.
The night makes a gradual retreat.
Dawn comes in under a shade,
strikes his desk
approves the slow advance of wonder.

February

Walking with you again
spring makes her shy voice heard
it is time
for brooks to bubble under ice
the steady drip drip of winter
crying out her last sad days.

It is late February
and crocuses are weeks away
but I wake in the night
to the absurdity of thunderstorm
and out of this season
our hands shoot out
like new stalks
driving toward green beginnings.

October

The sky slipped down
bunching in corners
like a blanket
around the contours of sleep.
They felt it between them
pressing the high grass
into a message
rolled back in waves
across the splintering field.
All was seed pods and floating
milkweed tops scattering
at a touch,
clouds cantering across the sky.

The day rippled.

They lay down
in a space of brown grass
dried and made small
by the push of wind.
The sky got bigger and bigger
the bare trees revealing two crows
big as balloons
and the big open branches
greeting the wayward sun.

Moving Through Time

This slow train
of our lives
moving through time together
a local
where each window
frames another scene
from the past—
the birth of a child,
the anniversary of desire
and the stops resound
with a clattering of memories
those things we knew once
now faded like old fabrics
left too long in the sun.
We try to get used
to the ride
knowing there are no stops
for us
this is the train you board
only to watch destinations
passing you by.
And holding hands
stiffening to the jolts of time
we know what it is
to be a little afraid
and yet to follow
this fixed path
like the sun
moving toward darkness
with an unchecked love
of the day.

A Poem

A poem is a private gift
publicly given.
It finds a way
crossing the mountains of an era
to take up residence in the future.
Art prefers
the elegance of the timeless.
But poets look over
the shadows of the day
lengthening into mortal harm
and declare their love
for particular people
hair graying
answering the summons of decay
and they make
in their small ways
something for one person
rather than the world
to remember.

The Voice in Poetry

"It's the voice,"
you tell me
shedding your winter underwear
on this March day.
It's warm after all
and you sweat in the many layers
you have brought.
"Too much poetry sounds the same.
Even when there's a good one,
it isn't true of a whole collection."
You have taken off your watch
and strung your wedding ring
on the strap like a worry bead.
I often see it
while we're making love.
"There has to be a really wide range."
Now you have lain down
next to me and we listen
to the walkers in the apartment upstairs.
Once again we begin
to trace out through surface veins
the future of an afternoon.
"It's not like that with your poetry,"
kissing me
"It sounds different all the time."

Love Poem

Some days in the library
I spend an hour
looking for a poem for you
in all the poetry books, unopened
looking like new
wanting some really good love poem
to xerox for you.
If I find one
I slide it over
the edge of your desk
until it touches your hand.
Today I have bad luck
in the books.
There is only one thing to do:
I sit in an oak-paneled room
writing a poem to you.

The Moblile

For my birthday you
made me a mobile:
black fish straining
their thin forms
on stiff vaulted hooks.

When you came
you kissed me once,
then chided me for taste.
It seems as if
I'd hung the mobile
in a way that marred
its grace: one limb
twisted like a broken flyer.

You performed sure
surgical adjustments.
In the hovering silence
of my room
the fish float free.

The Heart's Terrain

There is a place
inside the heart
that has known nothing
but silence
leaning into an uncut wind
like tundra.
The busy world
revolves around it.
But inside
it is like looking out
through a two way mirror
seeing those strangers
trading the baggage of the day
for tokens of redemption
and knowing
they do not see you.

The place has been silent
for a long time
used to a landscape without form
knowing itself only
through the edges of emptiness and ice
the boundaries unmarked.
But one day
under an arctic sun
someone arrives at the place.
A hand reaches out to touch
stirring the astonished air.

Beginning Again

Like a slow season
beginning to wake
the dark limbs
shading to green
like the surface ice of ponds
waiting to crack
I move out again
to find a feeling
that will ease this pain
lift me off this reef
this frozen barrier
silent like a zero zone
pulsing with the erratic rhythm
of the numb heart.
It is cold with disquiet
breeding such hard remarks
our shared silences
mirrors turning inward
reflecting the self's cold stare.
But I can feel
the wind change
the bitterness lose its edge
and moving slowly closer
we put our backs to the dying season
and wait for warmth
watching for signs of the thaw.

A *Wedding Poem*

This day
the small places
inside the heart
grow bolder:
There is room here
on the inside for more
than the mind imagined.
The small places
begin breathing
making themselves bigger
opening out
on the wide expanse of union.
This day
you watch the sun
tilt into summer
growing hotter
with the season's bright harvest
of hope.
Easing your way
into being more than one
testing the depths of perception.
It is too late now
to go back.
You are known.
The distance which secured your past
gave you a voice for saying no
is suddenly not far away
but close
like a path taken together.

There is a time
near the end of the day
twilight hazing the summer
when it is no longer day
but not yet night.
It is a time of transition
and you make love then
darkness drawn over you,
a cloak of love.
You sense your whole wardrobe
is changing.

About the Author

Richard Meade was born in 1946 in Clinton, Iowa, and grew up in the suburbs of Chicago. He has attended Earlham College, Clark University, and The University of Chicago, where he is currently completing a Ph.D. in American literature. While an undergraduate, he edited *Crucible*, a college literary magazine. In 1972 he was a winner of the first annual Worcester Poetry Festival. The same year his pamphlet, *Portage Lake and Other Poems* was published. It was the first of the Gob Poetry Series which later included David Holliday and Joseph Langland. His work has appeared in the literary magazines. This is his first book. Mr. Meade now lives in Riverside, Illinois with his wife, Laura.

P. O. Box 10040
Chicago, Ill. 60610

Story Press is a small, non-profit publishing company primarily devoted to the short story. The *Chicago Tribune* says, "Story Press should be praised." Our Illinois Writers Series has been called "a series to watch" by *Publishers Weekly* and our books have won several literary awards. We have recently begun to publish some poetry.